DOUBLE TAKE

poems by

Paloma Yannakakis

Finishing Line Press
Georgetown, Kentucky

DOUBLE TAKE

ACKNOWLEDGMENTS

Many thanks to the following journals and publishers, where the following poems first appeared:

"Song Divides Itself" was previously titled "The Scattered Song" in *Green Mountains Review*
"To Touch Blood on Stone" in *Contemporary Tangential Surrealist Poetry: An Anthology* (SurVision Books)

Publisher: Leah Huete de Maines
Editor: Christen Kincaid
Cover Art: 'Sun and Leaves IV' by David A Parfitt RI
Author photo: Mihalis Yannakakis
Cover Design: Elizabeth Maines McCleavy

Order online: www.finishinglinepress.com
also available on amazon.com

Author inquiries and mail orders:
Finishing Line Press
PO Box 1626
Georgetown, Kentucky 40324
USA

Table of Contents

*"I come too seldom down to the sea. But now I have come,
among good-sized stones with peaceful backs.
The stones have been gradually walking backwards out of the sea."*

—Tomas Tranströmer, "Slow Music"
(trans. Robert Bly)

Curriculum of Stones

Having taken a rough inventory of the landscape—
the local appearance of trees studding the mid-horizon
behind clouds that drift slowly
over the mountains on an otherwise clear day.

Casting off the eventual shipwreck of sight
as the only choice left to make:

if in ancient times the first cause was thunder, danger,
the second is harder to make out; ends perhaps in
a fist opening to clasp and unclasp
or a mouth to cry out,

as light is given to shine brightly no matter
the desolation it illuminates—

a curriculum of stones,
a concatenation, white
dispersed across the blue periphery,
vanish just as soon as they appear.

But there the sheep feed steadily on the grass,
and there a golden light over the mountains picks out
wheat's gold, and the rooster's crow
insists that time has passed.

There is nothing to suggest the landscape is
out of harmony with itself—

except myself looking,
except the one who names this wind
immaterial, imagines moving along the wall
like the shepherd anonymous in the fields,

the one who, between breaths, stops,
if only for a moment, to hear the sound of the waves
repeating, as if in that repetition
there was something else, too.

On the Beach

Like a shield or a body lying down,

                   : the range of choices beached on the shore. In

white plaster glaze we came upon the strange object
as on a rain-soaked field through which the rain
seeps unremitting

       On the white ladder going down, your mind
       a lion in a cage fighting off childhood wrongs, drafting
       some last act, becoming full with the taste of boredom.

       Then a tiny battalion of birds crossed low, close, to draw ribbons
of air on water indefinitely, the reflected sky

    Across each foaming wave line, you begin.
             The wind picks up your voice   and carries it.

Spurs

Hot spurs falling off the sun's disposition,
the old consortium dragging across the lawn.

A grazing deer lifts its head looking at me as I pass.
Waits to see if I mean to do it harm.

In the distance the park's amphitheater sits
in the round. Empty stage. Palladium pallor. And still
I can't help but wonder at the scope of it, like an actor

who lifts his arm before the curtain falls once more,
compelled to ask in what direction he falls.

My bones, my flesh, know the ring of it—
whatever I was seeking, I've forgotten it now.

I lay down there in that milding light
at the border, listening
for gaps in the wind. Quiet, then not.

Hills sloping in either direction,
it passes through me without stopping.

Song Divides Itself

Wading into a widening field, it becomes harder to remember...
in the name of—*what?*—had he promised to forget? And in what
moment had he made that promise, relinquishing the measure of
the fields, and the suffering, the suffering forgotten with the song,
the song now some spurious notes scattered here and there,
gathering in distant splendor,   —and everything dividing,
expendable in the already divided day. The sound of an animal dying
grows to a desperate pitch. And everything beside remains.

The Moth

The moth has long stopped
    scraping against the window. I watch it
climb up the pane of glass.
A little light escapes from underneath
    its folded wings.

I don't know anymore
the part I like less: the one that was willing
    to go so far, or the one that kept going
despite everything—as if that
    final distinction, heaped
upon the occasion, made—or could

make all the difference. Like someone
    balancing on the river's edge noticing
a frail etching of ice hanging on
    to the shallow banks.

The harder of the two still beating,
the way across a field the sun
    seems to burst as it breaks
unevenly through clouds, passing
    inside and through as if coming
from a great distance to arrive on
    the page you are currently reading.

We want to be what we've always been,
  only changed—limbs laid bare
until they split apart, facing skyward,
  until it is impossible to look away.

Admit what's beyond rescue and
leave it, finally, to its own devices—

the way a desperate person believes
  what they love is saved because
that which was destroyed
  cannot be destroyed again.

What Mastery Leaves Behind

Give me the body that has lived under
that thought: the ruined body,
hollow flexion on the scattered grounds
of speech—that if it dared in haste,

dared too much, whistling in the high
branches or bowled-over in gray horror at
the devastation below, falls past the point
where a flock of birds might shun the wintery

fields thickened to a standstill and
keep fear in check, that double-breasted
beast hammering in the far-away-
near at his heels that lie beside the earth

in perfect silence, small ripple inside the wind,
having turned back to find the same interior
now matches the exterior, you who would
make a stunted weapon of the blighted mass
and wield it light as ash in the open air.

What If the Landscape Keeps Going

A cold pocket of air fills my lungs.

If you'd asked me —

At the foot of the world,

a torn wreath. Accretion of feathers.

As if the birds arrived in winter unscathed.

I track their escape routes cast through rough equivalences of wind.

The snow that fell yesterday builds a tunnel from today to tomorrow.

I yell across it, but no one answers. We hoisted our flags long ago.

Impossible to tell if one cavalry is arriving or readying to depart.

When I've verified that no one is going to come, I surrender to
the imprints on the other side, trying
not to slip.

Crouching down, I pick up a branch,
snap it in two, just to hear the sound.

Always the habitual places and precise, remembered gestures.

But the landscape keeps going, doesn't wait for an answer,
ends in a village that can only be seen from
the ridge of an outermost hill   where an abandoned amphitheater
overgrown with grass
lies, marble seats intact, in the ochre and blue on that hill-
side
rushing down together —

We were trying to say something through the wind.

The animal that you were, shorn of all its attributes, walks on.

Notes for Recognition (One More Shore)

1. Between two stones
the record of our address: cuts carved
on the side of the wind,
aria arrested / a return to life?

Black crickets touching up
the edges.

2. I pull the quiet lever. Separate out
the formal difference.

This is what I imagine
death sounds like: a pattern of unidentifiable
sounds,
objects with no future—

soft where they should be
hard, broken
at the corners—something interrupted,

that could have (should have)
been a weapon...

3. Tension of the hand that loses itself in the phrasing
Whaled in the boundary of an eye.

4. To see me in the moment before
I recognize *you*—

5. Furthermore, we wanted to be whole.

Landscape with a Calm

Wandering in the king's gardens,
    the feeling he's been there before: echo-location
beside the lifeless moss and mating pigeons. Like a scene in which
    all the façades have come down without the usual
flourishes. This far from the source,
    though it looks branded in certainty, ceremonial
even—a steeple and crowded trees in the distance
    suddenly waving over the blue sky as if freshly planted,
straining against silence, sword against which
    at long last he had declined to fall; no more
to lay claim to the bitter reeds twisting
    aimlessly in the wind and the ragged fire within, the whole of it
bearing down with each flick of the wrist
    —now you see it, now you don't—
as the landscape streamed past him, for what use is
    a pointed spear, the owner
having outgrown its purpose?
    Between the score and the performance,
the message fell past, bannerless —
    the particulars recollected in pools of
disappearing acts... just so, he sat
    suspended in thought, a mind
led out to pasture next to a grove of
    olive trees and a circular lake of green water decorated with
a metal filigree border, now rusting, when he realized that
    a wild dog had been staring at him from across the lake
the entire time.

It must be somewhere between grace and
recklessness to learn what there is to be destroyed only when
    it's half-destroyed, he thought, looking up at the wall
in ruins. The light there is so beautiful, it's almost
    enough to forget. *I don't know what the going's good for*
but while it's good, I'll go, he whispers to the dog.
    Better to keep one's hands raised than
to resist. Just as a wave or
    a flower demands to be seen, to form
an unbroken line with the horizon.

Sweet Not Allways

"EVEN THE ONE WHO WORKED FOR IT IS DEAD"
read the sign on the figural coffins

this labor is not beautiful
but it fills the empty vessels

in the last district
practicing

                    a form of attention
                    mannered &
                    mundane

on the way down   availed myself
of its slow stammer   stumbling free

listen: we're far from
any place one would call home

if they find me here   thought without grammar
ruled out   black on black sieve

siloed without salvo

discarded parts overturned
in a snowed-over field

all gentleness revoked:

the horse's back was wide enough
to plant myself there

To Touch Blood on Stone

I readied myself in the rain.

How much forgetting it takes
   to remember, your mouth

now curving around
a question incinerated
   at the root. Hold it

close to the hilt, the mandrake's
shriek when it's torn from the ground
   for good. I waited

a long time to hear the echo
descend in diminished stops,
   through rooms too numerous to count.

The bird in movement goes on
   forever landing.

Negative Sublime

Edged into what should be forgotten,
the blank night unfolding its cliffs

miles away from the nearest shore

I said that time stood still
and meant it,

clasped at the center of its unfolding
the waters poured

dismay or abandon making its way slowly
across the countryside, a few pockets of shells

    filling the narrows,

              flattening in the mind's eye, a stone thrown over
the illegible edge,

              sound falling free of its intention—

who sings below this rock
in the shapeless underbrush?

    an array of shales juts off
    the cliff,
          bluer than oncoming night—

blue-black sky a swerve I walked up
the hill to see the white blow-up
doll outside the gallery thrashing in the wind, limbs
splayed in all directions

while spectators tended to fear
like an endangered species,

    the proper angle
        of correction
           riven in grey-brown dustfields;

spent time like a break-in
in excess of myself,

and then it is easy to forget
I am singing to you—

Double Take

I woke up, a ceremony unfolding past the hedge.
Overgrown ear, and there consideration flew
out the window. Doubling back
from where I came,
collected the shreds of doubt like second skin,
held in their sleeve, a cut willow.

Take the count, white thrush, limed line.
Like the bees that build a bridge with their bodies,
body-to-body, to cross gaps in the terrain.

In widening circles the understory it lasted
a storied while   as if there unleavened
sky existed   or there   whatever arises   rose
from the ashes   all the lifelong
day driven to distraction   out of the air
a blister of sound cored   in the cave
of its recognition   We walked
to the edge of seeing and spied on ourselves
next to vast repertoires
action adjacent.

L'Avventura

We come back from the small struggle
only to face the big one.
In the days when nothing
could divide us, we looked for signs, old school,
by the stars, carried on by the surefooted waves.
Days decline now against chance, lie thrashed
on the threshold, driven against rock wall.

The same fact uttered twelve years apart
survives intact, unlike
all the rest. Why, then, saying it once
isn't enough? You cried in the church
courtyard, inconsolable.

Nocturne

Startled into submission
in that hour of day when each thing seems fated
to slip into its actual self drips with the presence of
final things and the lights across the park are slowly
lit and unlit

                  I can almost see the sky from here.

As a body walking up from a field
then disappearing
                  or a face arriving is
something other than what was expected
in equal parts forgiving and unforgiving.

Blue

Before the storm catches up with itself,
before the finished brain succumbs
at the dry gate of its ambition,
catch it heading off—

If I lay on the hard wet rock
   invisible to everyone but myself, if I
lurched from corner
  to corner answering the same
   call,
               took time,

spurned and speared its arrow, staggering
   this way and not that, knotted on
the cord of memory that resembles
             its motherless father,

Father, do you hear that? If I keeled
   against its dark oar without remorse
in the black night, heel to the wind, wonder
   dripping with jasmine beside

  the sea around which each thing looks more
like itself,

              — then, only the sea,

underneath
  it all was
          the undying desire to be
swallowed whole by the hotheaded waves.

I dreamt you died, and so, could not die again.

Three Tiers

Saw a man lift a white dog twice his size into his trunk like a baby.

Walking against the wind he waves to the dark next to
a water fountain no one is drinking from.

Three tiers on the ledger: an invisible waterfall, winding hills,
and the chalk on the board marking out time.

                                        I tried to draw the mountains

in Chile, in Greece, while the car angled
a curve at 80 mph
                        against the sultry water, jet black skies
exorbitant plunge

In central Mexico—
at the airport arriving, departing, on the outskirts of town
  suddenly there they are:

——

Time, the coin borrowed from another's mouth —

and the mountains I imagined
fleeing to sit at a wooden desk
breathing paper air

never materialized, though I ran towards them

I repeat the mountains in gaps, at intervals, the projector
sliding across the tongue of a darkened box.

Brackish in the wings of a song
I haul the stone slab higher

to build an inheritance
of negation

A bell inside the clock, chalk crumbled at your feet.

If I promise to make do (a design
without designs) straight as a river
(which is not)
                    a window then

a cut-out of sticks   what can be trusted to reliably
remember, driven as we are
to conclusion?

———

Finally took down the pastoral German etching of a couple
stopping at a mountain pass to admire the spring flowers
we found in an antique shop in Athens in the old part of town
waiting out a flood.

I haven't seen Mexico in 13 years, and the house that once
belonged to my family has since been torn down for
the expansion of a dentist's office.

——

Staghorn. Sumac. Corridor of silence.

A wall can be a cloud or a hammer,
thirst : or the illusion of thirst :

acrobatic, I ate of a false peace
then, as now

a quotation of hands
of clouds   simply to trace

the slope of the ground, passing

unevenly from one foot to the other,
  turning over   remembering the air

——

if for no other reason than to observe the versatile
grass and the damaged life of trees thrown

in all directions, in extremity

a double agent parsing the distance for clues
and the mild disguises lived off

 until each false portrait

runs its course, not to take arms
but armed   to lift

the stone in
exasperation   knees folded   ex
orbitant   as if it would expire

(in French *contour* translates as
accident of terrain or *(uncountable)*
relief   formal)

———

I give as I will and
what the years divide also comes back
ritournelle of daffodils and Siberian squill

This is the place I keep beside me
to be sung through to the end

the notes entering
and breaking, breaking

somewhere sorrowless and without censure
to partake of the parkour on whose island

the man now waving under diminished light
awake   in the specific gravity of his particular life
hurrying through

———

———

The soft density of trees reflected in a creek when you thought that all was lost.

It would have been easier perhaps not to see it.

5 P.M.

Everyone has gone.

Everyone that has touched this table is still here.

The object of the argument lost. No more

naked surrender. I waited

until silence broke its own back—

a canopy of trees for a sky.

That old refrain comes drifting through:

the future is a line of mountains

written in the dark.

Soak my feet in green paint before I go,

a red rag to wipe my sweat.

Everyone has gone.

Go on, play the music without notes.

Notes

"Song Divides Itself": the title is a phrase from Michael Palmer's *Notes for Echo Lake.*

"Double Take": "build a bridge with their bodies, body-to-body, to cross gaps in the terrain" is from the article, "A Journey into the Animal Mind," *The Atlantic*, March 2019, Ross Andersen.

With Thanks

The production of art is never a linear process and marked by innumerable influences—literary, artistic, and personal—extending far beyond this page.

But I would like to acknowledge some of my poet friends, whose presence has enriched my life. Special thanks to Amanda Auerbach and Jack Jung for their attentive reading and kind words that grace the back of this book, and for the attendant magic of their own writings. To Peter Myers, for his consummate eye and editorial wisdom; and to Anton Yakovlev, for his inimitable friendship.

Thanks to Neil Shephard for your mentorship; for showing me the way back to poetry after a long silence, now over a decade ago. And to Carl Phillips, for keeping the flame alive. To my teachers, especially Mark Levine and Elizabeth Willis, fellow workshop poets (you know who you are!) and novelists at the Iowa Writers' Workshop, where many of these poems were written–thank you for your encouragement and wisdom.

I am indebted to David A Parfitt RI, for generously giving me permission to use his beautiful monoprint as the cover for this book, and whose artwork I have the pleasure of seeing daily near my desk.

Finally, thank you to Finishing Line Press for taking a chance on these poems, and to my editor, Christen Kincaid.

I am grateful for my artistic collaborators and friends, Alyssa Gersony and Hannah Givler, for helping me see the possibilities of bringing writing to life beyond the page, which has no doubt changed my conception of the book-as-artifact for the better.

To my parents and family, for their love and support in all things.

Paloma Yannakakis is a Mexican-Greek-American poet. Her work has appeared in *Lana Turner, Washington Square, Denver Quarterly, Afternoon Visitor*, and other journals. She received her BA from Harvard College, a PhD in comparative literature from Cornell University, and an MFA in poetry from the Iowa Writers' Workshop. She serves on the editorial board of *House Mountain Review* and frequently collaborates with artists in other media. Her work has been supported by Hewnoaks and the Iowa Writers' Workshop. She currently lives and teaches in New York.

www.ingramcontent.com/pod-product-compliance
Lightning Source LLC
Chambersburg PA
CBHW022051080426
42734CB00009B/1301